It's You & Me, Mom'

It's You & Me, Mom

25 Cool Devotions for Moms & Kids

Greg Johnson

BROADMAN
& HOLMAN
PUBLISHERS

Nashville, Tennessee

Printed in the United States of America

4253-94
0-8054-5394-6

Published by
Broadman & Holman Publishers
Nashville, Tennessee

Acquisitions and Development Editor: Janis Whipple
Interior Design & Production: Desktop Miracles, Inc.

Dewey Decimal Classification: 242.2
Subject Heading: DEVOTIONAL LITERATURE
Library of Congress Card Catalog Number: 95-43036

Unless noted otherwise, Scriptures are from the Holy Bible,
New International Version, copyright © 1973, 1978, 1984
by International Bible Society.

Library of Congress Cataloging-in-Publication Data

Johnson, Greg, 1956–
    It's you and me, Mom : 25 cool devotions for moms and kids /
Greg Johnson.
        p.   cm.
    ISBN 0-8054-5394-6 (pbk.)
        1. Parenting—Religious aspects—Christianity—Meditations.
2. Parents—Prayer-books and devotions—English.   3. Children—
Religious life.   4. Devotional calendars.   I. Title.
BV4529.J636   1996
249—dc20   95-43036
                                                          CIP

96 97 98 99 00 5 4 3 2 1

To Troy and Drew,
That you may know Jesus—and your mom!

Moms, Read This

Yes, it's tough to find the time to work on a book like this with your child, but the few total hours it will take to complete could pay dividends for years to come. Once you get started, you probably won't even have to coax your child or remind him it's time to do another section. Why? Because with all of the rewards built in, he'll *want* to complete it . . . fast!

But don't let him go *too* fast. Make sure he understands each passage. Most importantly, get ready to take a trip down memory lane. You'll find yourself recalling things about your own grade school days you thought you had forgotten years ago. When you're done with this book, your child will know exactly what you were like when you were his age!

Feel free to go through the suggested rewards (on pp. 107–110) and do some adjusting if they aren't strong motivators for you and your child to move through the book. Space is provided for you to write in what rewards you think would be best.

How long should it take you to get through this book? There's no set amount of time. It should take between ten to twenty minutes per section. Most moms probably have time for about three to five sections per week. Don't feel rushed—and don't rush. Let the lessons sink in, and help your child apply what you're learning.

Finally, though each section should relate to any child in the third through sixth grade, don't worry about skipping a section or two if your child can't relate to the subject. That will just get him to the rewards a little faster! Or, if you're finding that most of the lessons don't apply, put this book down for a year or two until they do.

Kids, Read This

You're about to take an adventure through part of the Bible. OK, so it probably won't be as fun as Disney World. But what's fun about this adventure is, you get to take your mom with you. You can't do it alone. Along the way, as you both complete a number of sections, there are prizes and rewards!

The goal of this book is for you and your mom to go through together fifteen passages from the life of Christ and ten passages from Proverbs, find out what each passage says, and, especially, discover what it means. Your mom will be asking you some questions—some will be easy; others will require a little thought. But hey, you're up for a challenge, aren't you?

Another goal is for you to learn what your mom was like when she was your age. Does she tell you stories about when she was a kid? If she doesn't, she will now! Feel free to ask her a lot of questions about how she handled each situation. You'll learn a lot!

How fast you go through this book is up to you. When you're done with each lesson and section, mark it off in the back of the book so you can check how close you are to the next reward! You're the scorekeeper in this adventure!

The best time to remind Mom to sit down with you alone is probably after dinner or right before bed. You set the schedule with her so it works out best for both of you.

Are you ready? Then grab a pencil while Mom reads the rules ... and get going!

The Rules of the Game

Before you get started, Mom, let's talk about how each lesson is set up.

"It's Alive." You or your child can read the passage. It doesn't matter who does it.

"Let's Dig." In this section there are five questions to ask your child. Some require thought, some are the yes-and-no variety, and some invite you to help your child find the answer. If your child gets stuck on any of them, either answer them yourself or move on to the next one. Some questions may be over the head of a second or third grader, but hopefully not too many.

"Mom's Turn." This is where your child asks *you* the questions. The goal is for you to try to remember stories and feelings you had as a grade schooler. If you honestly can't relate to the question or can't remember a situation, move on to the next one. If other stories come to mind that *almost* relate to the topic, tell them. Talking about your past is the goal.

"What if . . . ." It's your child's turn again to think. You read the situation, making sure he understands what's happening, and then ask him the questions. Sometimes there's one situation; sometimes more. If you're good at thinking up "what if" situations, and you can think of something that may apply better to your child, then by all means use it.

"Now What?" This may be the most important part: application. Now's your chance to teach your child the life skill of applying passages from the Bible. Again, if what's written doesn't help him apply the passage, think of something else that will.

"Overtime Challenge." If you have enough time (and your child wants to earn bonus points), open your Bible, read the passages, and answer the question. This should help shed some more light on the opening verses and generate more discussion.

"Plant It Deep" or "Pray It Up." Some sections end with a verse to memorize, others with a prayer to pray. The memorization is optional; but, again, your child will earn extra points (and more rewards) by memorizing it. If your time has run out, you can both memorize it separately at a later time and then recite it before the next section to still get credit. At the end of the book, there's a chance to review each memorized verse to earn extra points. The passages don't have to be word-perfect unless that's what you agree to. A good compromise is three helps.

Puzzles. After every five lessons there's either a crossword puzzle or a word search. The puzzles are fairly easy. The word searches could take some time. If you've got all but a couple of words, that's close enough. Just have fun doing the puzzles together.

Can this book be used for family devotions?

Sure! If your children are close together in age and Dad wants to be involved—go for it. All you have to do is make some decisions about how the points are kept (or perhaps not keeping them at all). Then when you ask the questions for kids and read the "What If" situations, try to get everyone to respond. When it's "Mom's Turn," have Dad answer, too. Not every question will apply to him, but that's OK. Just try to keep the lesson moving so the kids don't get bored.

Contents

Section Four

Section Five

Appendices

1

Give It Up—and
Don't Take It Back!

It's Alive

*"Who of you by worrying can add a single hour to his life?
Since you cannot do this very little thing, why do you worry
about the rest?"* (Luke 12:25-26)

Let's Dig

1 Name four things you have worried about most:

- _____   • _____

- _____   • _____

2 How did worrying help in those situations?

3 What is the best thing you can do to keep from worrying?

4 When you worry about something—especially after praying about it—what does that say to God?

5 Why do you think Jesus doesn't want us to worry about
things?

Mom's Turn

- Worry and fear are sometimes the same thing. When you were in grade school, what were some of your biggest fears or worries?

- How about when you hit your teen years? What did you worry about then? Do you ever remember a time when worrying helped in a certain situation?

- Now that you're a mom, you have a whole new set of problems to think about. What do you find yourself worrying about most, and how are you able to turn those things back over to God and really trust that He's in control?

What If . . .

. . . your family had to move to another town in the middle of the school year. At your old school you had tons of friends, but now you have to start all over. The night before your first day, you pray with your mom and dad about finding new friends and fitting in.

Will you be able to sleep very well that night, or will you lie awake wondering if God is going to come through?

How about your first day? Will you be nervous or confident that God will answer your prayer?

. . . it's the day of your final baseball game for the championship of the whole city. As one of your team's top hitters, you know your teammates are counting on you to do well. The past five games or so, however, you haven't gotten one clean hit . . . and you've struck out eight times! You're trying your best, but you're worried you'll let the team down.

How can you overcome your fear of not playing well?

Is God concerned more about the game or about your attitude? (Or is He equally concerned about both?)

Now What?

Think about the week ahead. Name two things coming up that have the chance of making you worry most. Now find two pieces of paper and write those worries down, one on each piece.

Mom, pray about those two things. (Go ahead, right now!)

It's Mom's turn. Mom, you write down two things that you could worry about this week. Then have your child pray about them for you.

Now that you've turned those two worries over to God, it's important that you not take them back and start to worry again. Mom, you take your child's two "worry papers" and put them in your Bible and remember to pray about them this week. Then give your two "worry papers" to your child to put in his Bible.

Remember, you don't need to worry about them anymore because the other person—and God—are taking care of them.

Overtime Challenge (150 points)

- Philippians 4:6–7. What happens when you pray rather than worry?

- John 14:27. Whose peace should you want most of all?

- Isaiah 26:3. What do you have to do to have God's peace?

Plant It Deep (150 points)

"You will keep in perfect peace him whose mind is steadfast, because he trusts in You." (Isaiah 26:3)

Praying for Stones and Snakes

It's Alive

"Which of you, if his son asks for bread, will give him a stone? Or if he asks for a fish, will give him a snake? If you, then, though you are evil, know how to give good gifts to your children, how much more will your Father in heaven give good gifts to those who ask Him!" (Matthew 7:9–11)

Let's Dig

1 Is this saying we will get whatever we ask for?

2 When you ask for ice cream, the newest Nintendo game, permission to spend the night at someone's house, or the latest clothes, are you always asking for a "good gift"?

3 Would your parents be good parents if they gave you whatever you asked for?

4 Since God wants to give us good gifts and He loves to answer our prayers, does that mean He should give us whatever we pray for, even if He knows it's not really a "good gift"?

5 Would God be a good God if He gave us everything we asked for?

Mom's Turn

- What were some things you wanted from your parents (really badly) but they would **never** give to you? Looking back, do you now think your parents were wise to withhold what you asked for?

- Have you ever prayed for something you thought was "bread," but had God given it to you, it would have been "a stone"? Were you glad God didn't give it to you?

- How do you know whether things you pray for are "fish" or "snakes"?

What If . . .

. . . you ask your mom to give you a motorcycle for your birthday. You really want one badly, you'd take care of it better than anything you've ever owned before, and you'd even do your chores and homework before riding it. Unfortunately, you are five years away from being old enough to have a license, and your feet can barely reach the footrests. Plus, you don't have a garage in which to store it at night.

Would your mom be a good mom if she said, "OK, I'll get the motorcycle, and we'll just hope nothing happens to you or the bike"?

Why or why not?

. . . you continually ask God to show you the person you will one day marry. All through grade school and into junior high you wonder who it could be. Finally, you think you find the one. This person likes you too, and you become boyfriend and girlfriend. But in the middle of your seventh grade year, your love moves away to another state—for good.

Is God a bad guy for not answering this prayer the way you wanted? Or is this type of request something God knew wouldn't be good for you to know the answer to while you're young?

Now What?

In your life you'll pray about things that won't always get answered the way you want. Because God loves us, and because He knows the future better than us, He'll sometimes say no (or wait) to things that really seem (to you) like a good gift. He may say no to making the team, getting an "A" on a math test . . . or even healing your grandma from cancer.

How does it make you feel for God to say no to good stuff like that?

It all boils down to whether you can trust that God knows what He's doing. Name a few little things that are easy to trust God in. Then name a few big things that may be a little tougher—situations in which you have to say, "I don't understand it, but I know You know what's best."

Easy Stuff	Tough Stuff

This is just like trusting your parents, isn't it? You don't hate them just because they don't give you what you think you need—you learn to deal with it. You learn to realize they love you more than anyone else and only want what's *really best* for you.

Overtime Challenge (150 points)

- James 1:5–8. What's a condition for praying?
- James 4:3. What's another condition?
- 1 John 3:21–22. And another?

Pray It Up

Dear Heavenly Father, I know that You're a good God who loves to give good gifts. I also realize that sometimes the things I ask for are pretty selfish. Help me to trust You and believe that You would never want to give me a snake, but that You always want to give good gifts that would really make my life better. Amen.

3

Keeping Your Balance

It's Alive

And Jesus grew in wisdom and stature, and in favor with God and men. (Luke 2:52)

Let's Dig

1 When you think about growing up, what are the first things that come to mind?

2 Everyone "grows up" in at least four different ways. Growing up in wisdom means using and exercising your mind. How do you do that, and how are you doing?

3 Growing up in stature means getting taller and keeping your body in shape. How do you do that, and how are you doing?

4 Growing up "in favor with God" means doing what you can to get to know Jesus Christ better. How do you do that, and how are you doing?

5 Growing up "in favor with ... men" means being a good friend to others (not having a lot of friends). How do you do that, and how are you doing?

Mom's Turn

- When you were growing up, were any of these areas neglected? Was there something you could have done to change that, or did your parents just not help you emphasize them?

- If you got out of balance by neglecting or over-emphasizing one or more of these areas, how did it affect you later in life?

- Even now as an adult it's sometimes easy to get out of balance. What areas do you still need to give more attention to in order to be in better balance?

What If . . .

. . . your two main goals in life are being a good student and being a good Christian. When you get good grades in school, your parents, grandparents, and teachers give you a lot of attention (sometimes even real rewards!). Spiritually, you rarely miss church or Sunday school, and you consistently read your Bible five times a week. The problem: You rarely exercise and don't have many friends.

Is your life out of balance? What should you do to change?

. . . all you really care about are sports and friends. You're a good athlete in nearly everything you try, and because you're good, a lot of people want to hang around with you. Your after-school time is spent practicing either at school or with friends in the neighborhood. Athletics has made you popular; but, to you, church and school are both boring.

Is your life out of balance? What should you do to change?

Now What?

It's easy to be involved in things that give us immediate rewards (like athletics and friends) and just as easy to neglect things that help us over the long haul (like school and our relationship with God).

Together with Mom, figure out if any of these four areas are being neglected or over-emphasized. If they are, what's it going to take for you to build habits that will put you back in balance?

Pick *one* area you can begin to work on today.

Overtime Challenge (200 points)

- 1 Corinthians 3:16–17. If your body is God's temple, what should you do and not do to keep it in good working condition?

- Proverbs 18:24. What are some qualities of a good friend?

- Colossians 3:2. How do you set your mind on things above?

- 1 Peter 1:13. Why is it important to have a ready mind?

Pray It Up

Dear Lord, it's hard to keep all four of those areas in balance, but I want to be just like You. Help me not to neglect one of those areas and become less than what You want me to be. Show me how to grow more in wisdom and stature and in favor with You and others. Amen.

What Do You
Love Most?

It's Alive

Yet at the same time many even among the leaders believed in Him [Jesus]. But because of the Pharisees they would not confess their faith for fear they would be put out of the synagogue; for they loved praise from men more than praise from God. (John 12:42–43)

Let's Dig

1. Do you know people who say they know Jesus or go to church but are afraid to let others know about it?

2. What are they afraid will happen?

3. Do you sometimes feel afraid to let people know you go to church?

4. What's the worst thing they would do to you?

5. How would that make you feel?

Mom's Turn

- If you were a Christian while growing up, talk about what happened when people found out you went to church. Do you think your child has it easier, harder, or about the same as you did?

- Today how do people who aren't in the church respond to you when they find out you're a Christian? How do you feel?

- Why are you so much more able to stand up under the pressure now than when you were a kid?

What If . . .

. . . you're on a soccer team that sometimes has to go away on weekends to games and tournaments in other towns. When the coach talks about the schedule at the end of practice, he tells you there's a game this Sunday morning. He asks if everyone can make it.

What will you say?

. . . you tell your coach—in front of all the other players—that you have to go to church and won't be able to come to the game. Your teammates give you a hard time and tell you that you're letting the team down.

How does that make you feel? What will you say?

Now What?

Write down three situations in which others find out that you're a Christian or go to church.

- _____
- _____
- _____

Together with Mom, think about how you can respond in each situation so you don't feel ashamed, embarrassed, or funny about admitting it.

Overtime Challenge (150 points)

- Romans 1:16. How does not being ashamed of Jesus give you power?
- Romans 10:9-10. Why is it so important not to be ashamed of Jesus?
- Mark 8:38. Are there potential consequences for being ashamed of Jesus?

Plant It Deep (150 points)

I am not ashamed of the gospel, because it is the power of God for the salvation of everyone who believes: first for the Jew, then for the Gentile. (Romans 1:16)

5

Doing Stupid Stuff

It's Alive

Then the devil took him [Jesus] to the holy city and had Him stand on the highest point of the temple. "If You are the Son of God," he said, "throw Yourself down. For it is written: 'He will command His angels concerning you, and they will lift you up in their hands, so that you will not strike your foot against a stone.'"

Jesus answered him, "It is also written: 'Do not put the LORD your God to the test.'" (Matthew 4:5–7)

Let's Dig

❶ Does God need to perform circus stunts to prove His existence? (Does He need to prove anything?)

❷ Why do kids sometimes dare someone to do something?

❸ Do you ever need to do stupid stuff on dares to prove *anything?*

❹ Satan tried to twist Scripture to get Jesus to do something stupid. What did Jesus do when Satan challenged Him?

❺ Are you the type who will take a dare if someone gives you one, or are you the type to know when something is stupid?

Mom's Turn

- Can you remember when you took a dare from someone that was really dumb? What did you learn from it?

- Why is putting God to the test a bad idea?

- When someone puts you to the test—to prove something— what is that person really communicating? (How does it feel not to be trusted?)

What If . . .

. . . you and some friends were over at a construction site where they were building houses. One of the houses you explored didn't have glass on the windows or doors on the hinges. A neighbor kid dared you to jump from a second story ledge. You looked down and saw a mound of dirt about eight to ten feet below. It looked soft enough, but you weren't quite sure you wanted to do it.

What would you be thinking if all your friends called you a chicken?

What would it prove if you did wind up jumping?

What are the potential consequences for jumping?

. . . your cousin is coming with her family during Thanksgiving holiday. They don't go to church and her parents are having problems in their marriage. You really think it's time she look into what God could do in her life. The problem: you're too scared to ask!

Instead of overcoming your fear, you devise a little plan. If your cousin asks *you* about church on Sunday, you'll invite her to go. If not, then it must not be God's will.

Is this a good way to find out if God wants you to do something or not?

What would be an alternate plan?

Now What?

I'm sure you can see that putting yourself or God to foolish tests doesn't make much sense. It doesn't prove anything to anyone (except that you might be dumb enough to take a dare).

For you to realize that God is there and loves you—even if bad things do occasionally happen—what must God do to prove it? (Check all that apply.)

- ❏ Allow you to get lots of presents on your birthday and at Christmas.
- ❏ Always keep your parents safe and alive to take care of you.
- ❏ Put you in the popular crowd at school.
- ❏ Nothing—He's already done it.
- ❏ Make sure your parents are rich enough to pay for nice clothes for you.
- ❏ Allow you to do well in everything you try.
- ❏ Make sure you are never teased by others.

Overtime Challenge (200 points)

- Judges 6:36-40. Was this a good thing for Gideon to do, or was God putting up with Gideon's foolishness?
- Acts 1:12-26. How is this different than putting God to a test?

Pray It Up

Dear Lord, help me never to put You to a foolish test. Teach me to trust You no matter what happens. I realize that a simple trust in You is much better than making You do things to prove Your love for me.

When others try to put me to the test, help me not to give in to that type of pressure. I'm realizing the consequences can be too great for even just one wrong mistake. Amen.

Bonus Puzzle #1
(750 points)

ACROSS

2. "Do not be _____ about anything." (Philippians 4:6)

6. "'Do not let your hearts be _____.'" (John 14:27)

7. Who will be ashamed of us if we are ashamed of him? (Mark 8:38)

9. We are God's _____. (1 Corinthians 3:16)

10. Don't set your mind on _____ things. (Colossians 3:2)

12. "You will keep in perfect peace him whose mind is _____, because he trusts in you." (Isaiah 26:3)

14. If we lack wisdom, we should ask God, and He will give it to us _____. (James 1:5)

DOWN

1. If we lack _____ we should ask God. (James 1:5)

3. What two things should we not pray for? (Matthew 7:9–10)

4. We don't receive from God because we sometimes ask with wrong _____. (James 4:3)

5. Gideon used a _____ to find out what God's will was. (Judges 6:37)

8. "'Who of you by _____ can add a single hour to his life?'" (Luke 12:25)

9. Satan tried to _____ Jesus. (Matthew 4:6–7)

11. What should we never be ashamed of? (Romans 1:16)

13. "_____ your minds for action." (1 Peter 1:13)

6

How Solid Is
Your Rock?

It's Alive

"Therefore everyone who hears these words of Mine and puts them into practice is like a wise man who built his house on the rock. The rain came down, the streams rose, and the winds blew and beat against that house; yet it did not fall, because it had its foundation on the rock. But everyone who hears these words of Mine and does not put them into practice is like a foolish man who built his house on sand. The rain came down, the streams rose, and the winds blew and beat against that house, and it fell with a great crash." (Matthew 7:24-27)

Let's Dig

1. Since we can't actually hear Jesus speak words, which ones are we to put into practice?

2. Can we put them into practice if we don't read them and find out what they are?

3. How is reading about something and putting it into practice different?

23

④ What does the foundation for your house actually do? (Mom, you can help answer this if necessary.)

⑤ What "winds" (trouble and trials) blow into your life that can make your "house" (life) shake?

Mom's Turn

- When you were younger, which of these different "foundations" did most kids try to build their lives on:

family money	popularity	intelligence
sports	music	boyfriends/girlfriends
humor	alcohol/drugs	possessions (car, clothes)
faith in Christ	another religion	

- Did you try any of these "foundations"? Why?

- Some of these foundations "work" for a short period of time. Why is it important to have a foundation that will work for a lifetime?

What If . . .

. . . your dad was in a car accident while you were at school. Your mom picked you up at noon, told you about the accident, and said he may not live. Suddenly you've got a major "wind" blowing through your life. Which foundation of those mentioned above in the "Mom's Turn" section will help you through this?

Can you or Mom think of any promises from the Bible which would help give you comfort and strength?

. . . one day, you and two of your best friends are walking home from school. On the way you stop at one of their homes to play Nintendo. Your friend's parents aren't home, and instead of playing video games he pulls out some cigarettes he stole from his mom. He says he's tried smoking them and it's no big deal. All three of you go out back and before you know it, both of them have lit the cigarettes and are telling you to try it. You know what the Bible says about how to treat your body, and you know your parents wouldn't approve.

What would you do?

How does having a foundation of right and wrong help you make the correct decision?

Now What?

Write down six things that test (or would test) your foundation as a Christian more than anything else:

- _____
- _____
- _____

- _____
- _____
- _____

Strengthening your foundation is a constant process. How could your foundation grow stronger so that you're ready to withstand any "wind" that comes your way?

What could happen to your life if you didn't have a strong foundation?

Overtime Challenge (150 points)

- 2 Timothy 3:14–17. Why is the Bible such a good source of material for building your foundation?

- 2 Corinthians 11:24–27. How did Paul's relationship with Jesus help him through so many trials?

Plant It Deep (150 points)

"Therefore everyone who hears these words of Mine and puts them into practice is like a wise man who built his house on the rock." (Matthew 7:24)

7

Can You Be Trusted?

It's Alive

"Whoever can be trusted with very little can also be trusted with much, and whoever is dishonest with very little will also be dishonest with much." (Luke 16:10)

Let's Dig

1 Should trust be given away freely, or should it be earned?

2 How can you earn trust?

3 How does dishonesty make you untrustworthy?

4 What does it mean to be trustworthy?

5 Is being trusted in small things so you can be trusted with bigger things important to you?

Mom's Turn

- When you were growing up, were there times your parents couldn't trust you? What had you done?

- What were the benefits you experienced when you were trusted? What were the consequences when you weren't?

- How important is it for you to trust your child? Are there benefits and consequences?
- What do you think it means to have God trust you?

What If . . .

. . . in the morning before you left for school, your mom asked you to rake the leaves and clean the garage when you got home. Instead, you went over to a friend's house and helped him organize his baseball cards. Arriving back home just before dinner, you walked in the door and told your mom you wanted to get a paper route so you could earn more money (to get your baseball card collection up to speed with your buddies').

Are you really ready for a big responsibility like that?

How should your parents handle the situation?

. . . you're invited to a sleepover by someone at school. Your parents don't know the family very well, but agree to let you go. You check with your friend and are assured there won't be any R-rated videos. You tell your parents that if there are raunchy videos, you'll call them to have them come pick you up.

When you get home the next day, you tell your parents that there was one video that was pretty bad, but you went into another room and did other stuff instead of watching it. You would have felt embarrassed had you had to call your parents and leave.

Do you think you built your parents' trust or tore it down?

Mom, was that a trustworthy thing for your child to do?

Would there have been a better option?

Now What?

With your mom, make a list of things that you do (or can do) that either tear down their trust for you or make it stronger.

Tears Down Trust	Builds Trust

Overtime Challenge (150 points)

- Proverbs 11:28. What should you *not* trust in?

- 1 Corinthians 1:9. Can God be trusted?

- 1 Timothy 1:12. Why was being faithful important to Paul?

Plant It Deep (150 points)

"Whoever can be trusted with very little can also be trusted with much, and whoever is dishonest with very little will also be dishonest with much." (Luke 16:10)

8

It's the Heart
That Counts

It's Alive

*"What do you think? There was a man who had two sons.
He went to the first and said, 'Son, go and work today in the
vineyard.'*

*"'I will not,' he answered, but later he changed his mind
and went.*

*"Then the father went to the other son and said the same
thing. He answered, 'I will, sir,' but he did not go.*

"Which of the two did what his father wanted?"

"The first," they answered. (Matthew 21:28–31a)

Let's Dig

1 Why do you think the first son changed his mind?

2 Why did the second son lie to his father when he probably
knew he wasn't going to do the work?

3 What is the difference between "obeying on the *outside*"
and "obeying on the *inside*"?

4 Which way does God (as well as your parents) want you
to obey?

5 Why is that hard sometimes?

Mom's Turn

- In what were you most and least obedient to your parents while you were growing up?

- Why is obedience from the heart so important?

- Why do you think some kids are obedient and others aren't?

What If . . .

. . . your parents tell you not to run in parking lots where there are a lot of cars.
Why do they want you to obey?

. . . your teacher at school says that fighting on the playground will not be tolerated.
What could happen if you disobey?
Why would the school have a rule like this?

. . . the policeman at your school assembly tells you that, even though you're just on your bike, you must obey the traffic signs just as though you were in a car.
What is his motive for telling you to obey the laws?
What could the consequences of disobedience be?

. . . your parents tell you not to accept rides from strangers unless they give you the secret password you've worked out together with them in case of emergencies.
What are the potential consequences if you don't obey?

Now What?

Obeying from the heart is one of the toughest lessons we have to learn in life. But whether it's God or other authorities over us (parents, teachers, etc.), obedience is one quality we can't afford to live without.

Name ten things you are asked to be obedient in:

* _____   * _____
* _____   * _____
* _____   * _____
* _____   * _____
* _____   * _____

If any of these are tougher to obey in (from the heart), talk about ways to do that so obeying would be easier.

Overtime Challenge (150 points)

* Ephesians 6:1–3. What are the benefits of obeying your parents?
* Hebrews 5:7–9. What are the benefits of Christ's obedience for us?
* John 14:21. What is the benefit of obeying God's Word?

Plant It Deep (150 points)

This is love for God: to obey His commands. And His commands are not burdensome. (1 John 5:3)

9

How Much Is Enough?

It's Alive

"What good is it for a man to gain the whole world, and yet lose or forfeit his very self?" (Luke 9:25)

Then Jesus said to His disciples, "I tell you the truth, it is hard for a rich man to enter the kingdom of heaven. Again I tell you, it is easier for a camel to go through the eye of a needle than for a rich man to enter the kingdom of God." (Matthew 19:23-24)

Let's Dig

1. Can people be unhappy even if they have nearly everything they want? How?

2. If you had a lot of wealth in this life, would you think about the next life? Why or why not?

3. Why do you think some people don't consider their life after death when they have a lot of the world's possessions?

4. Though it's not impossible to be rich *and* a Christian, Jesus said it was very difficult. How can someone keep possessions in their proper priority?

5 Do you ever struggle with wanting too many things?

Mom's Turn

- Was there ever a time in your life when making and having money or things took up most of your time? Did you think much about God during those times?

- Think of the wealthy people you have seen or heard about that aren't Christians. Why would they say they aren't interested in following Christ?

- What about now? Are you still tempted to pursue wealth rather than pursue God?

What If . . .

. . . you had a friend whose parents were very rich. The friend had almost anything he wanted, plus it seemed the family was always going on extravagant vacations. Though your friend had a lot of stuff, he was always wanting more; he never seemed content with what he had. Plus, he wasn't interested in church or God or anything.

What would you do or say to him to get him to consider that only God can really make someone happy, not things?

Now What?

Being content with what you have is one of the greatest possessions a person can own. Write down three ways you can learn to be more content with what you have so you won't ever have to worry about going "through the eye of a needle."

- _____
- _____
- _____

Overtime Challenge (200 points)

- Philippians 4:11–13. What is the process you must go through before you learn the secret of contentment? (Mom, you can help.)

- Hebrews 13:5. Why shouldn't you worry about money?

- 1 Timothy 6:6–10. Name four important facts from these verses.

1. _____ 2. _____

3. _____ 4. _____

Plant It Deep (150 points)

I have learned the secret of being content in any and every situation, whether well fed or hungry, whether living in plenty or in want. (Philippians 4:12b)

10

Would You Betray a Friend?

It's Alive

When evening came, Jesus was reclining at the table with the Twelve. And while they were eating, He said, "I tell you the truth, one of you will betray Me."

They were very sad and began to say to Him one after the other, "Surely not I, Lord?" (Matthew 26:20–22)

Let's Dig

1 Look up *betray* in the dictionary and try to understand what it really means.

2 How was Jesus betrayed?

3 Have you ever been betrayed by a friend?

4 How does it feel to be betrayed?

5 If you know the rest of the story, tell who else besides Judas turned his back on Jesus?

Mom's Turn

- Have you ever been betrayed by another friend? How did it feel?

- Have you ever betrayed Jesus by denying you knew Him? How?

- What do you think Jesus feels when we betray Him in one way or another?

What If . . .

. . . you're on the playground at school getting ready to play basketball with a few of your friends. Though you know your mom has to show up to talk to your sister's teacher, you don't think she'll come out on the playground to talk to you. But just as you're about ready to get in the game, she walks over to watch.

Though you see her, you don't let on that she's your mom. As she's getting ready to leave, one of the "cool" kids asks you if that's your mom. You ignore the question and start to get in the game.

What just happened?

Have you ever felt "embarrassed" to let others know who your parents are?

. . . it's your birthday, and for the party you decide to take your friends to a nearby roller skating rink. Your parents say you can only go if it's Christian music skate night.

About a dozen of your friends come, and after pizza, presents, and cake at your house, you head off to the rink. After about a half hour of skating, two of your friends make the comment that they can't recognize any of the music. They go ask the DJ, and he tells them they're only playing Christian music that night. They come back and ask you if you knew about that.

Will you be tempted to tell them you didn't know it was Christian skate night? Why or why not?

If you do tell them you didn't know, do you think that would be betraying Jesus ... or just lying?

Now What?

Admitting that you're a Christian or that you go to church can sometimes bring fear. You don't know what your friends will do or say, so it seems easier just to fudge on the truth instead of telling it like it is.

Name three situations, if you can, in which you are tempted to keep quiet—or lie—about whether you're connected with anything Christian:

- _____
- _____
- _____

With your mom, come up with things you can say to people in those situations that will help you tell the truth so you don't have to betray Jesus.

Overtime Challenge (150 points)

- John 6:61–65. Did Jesus still love the person who was going to betray Him?

- Matthew 27:3–5. When you betray someone—and you know you've done wrong—how can it make you feel?

- 2 Timothy 1:8. Why would anyone feel ashamed of letting others know what they believe?

Plant It Deep (150 points)

If you will stir up this inner power, you will never be afraid to tell others about our Lord ... (2 Timothy 1:8a, TLB)

Bonus Puzzle #2
(1,000 points)

```
E  R  N  D  N  A  S  U  F  F  E  R  I  N  G  F  K
H  O  I  L  U  F  H  T  I  A  F  A  R  B  D  O  P
A  C  S  C  Z  P  I  H  S  W  O  L  L  E  F  R  Y
N  K  O  E  C  R  P  E  R  D  A  N  G  E  R  F  D
T  Q  U  A  C  E  W  K  L  C  I  N  S  S  P  E  E
S  B  F  E  C  R  R  O  P  E  A  X  E  N  K  I  S
E  G  O  D  B  R  E  A  T  H  E  D  R  O  I  T  S
N  Y  U  N  O  L  C  T  I  C  N  E  V  I  M  U  A
O  L  N  P  E  C  K  S  W  O  J  P  I  S  O  D  R
H  E  D  M  G  E  E  A  H  M  P  P  C  S  S  E  R
S  Y  A  S  T  R  D  R  N  M  E  I  E  E  B  E  A
I  C  T  L  Y  P  I  L  V  A  Q  U  I  S  E  N  B
D  R  I  C  H  E  S  E  E  N  U  Q  Y  S  T  B  M
T  O  O  R  R  O  B  I  F  D  R  E  M  O  R  S  E
C  O  N  T  E  N  T  O  T  S  U  R  T  P  A  N  O
P  D  E  R  E  D  N  A  W  P  L  E  N  T  Y  T  B
```

BETRAY	FOUNDATION	ROCK
CAMEL	GOD-BREATHED	ROOT
COMMANDS	GRIEF	RUIN
CONTENT	HANGED	SAND
DANGER	NEEDLE	SECRET
DISHONEST	NEED	SERVICE
EMBARRASSED	OBEYS	SHIPWRECKED
EQUIPPED	PLENTY	SUFFERING
FAITHFUL	POSSESSIONS	TRUST
FELLOWSHIP	REMORSE	WANDERED
FORFEIT	RICHES	

Tickling Someone's Ears

11

It's Alive

"'These people honor Me with their lips, but their hearts are far from Me.'" (Matthew 15:8)

Let's Dig

1 How do you feel when someone tells you something they really don't mean?

____ betrayed   ____ unimportant   ____ lied to

____ mad   ____ hurt   ____ other _____

2 Can you recall a few times when you said something but didn't mean it?

3 Do you ever feel "pressured" to say things you don't mean in order to make someone else happy or keep the peace?

4 How do you think God feels when we say things to Him that He knows we really don't mean?

5 Why do you think it's important to always be honest with God? (Mom, you can help on this one.)

Mom's Turn

- When you were growing up, did you ever say things to your parents you didn't mean? Do you think they ever caught on?

- If you grew up in the church, did you ever feel the pressure to be the "nice Christian kid" and say all the right things? What did you do when that pressure hit?

- Ask your child if he sometimes feels "pressure" from you or Dad to behave a certain way. Next, let him know what you really want as it relates to his emerging relationship with God.

What If . . .

. . . your Sunday school teacher is going around the class and asking for everyone to tell about a time when God answered his prayers. While you know there is a God, and He's always watching out for you, you can't recall a specific answer to one of *your* prayers.

Each of the six people that answer before you mentions something. Now it's your turn.

Will you say something the teacher wants to hear, or will you tell the truth?

What do you think the other kids would believe about you if you told the truth? Should that matter?

Now What?

Trying to please others at the expense of the truth is a bad habit to get into. Pretty soon you tell people just what *you think* they want to hear instead of what you truly believe. You're actually telling the other person you don't respect or care for them enough to let him know the truth.

Name topics that are tough for you to talk about honestly with God or your parents.

- _____   - _____
- _____   - _____
- _____   - _____

Together with Mom, discuss ways you can feel more comfortable saying things you really believe on each of these issues.

Overtime Challenge (150 points)

- Colossians 3:9–10. Why shouldn't you lie?

- Proverbs 26:24–26. Is a person always able to hide what he really believes?

- Jeremiah 9:4–6. How do you learn not to tell the truth?

Pray It Up

Dear Heavenly Father, it's tough sometimes always to tell the truth, especially when people I care about might be hurt by it. But I know how important truth is to You. I know You would rather have my lips match what I really believe than for me not to be honest—especially with You. Help my mouth always to speak the truth. Amen.

12

Who You Gonna Call?

It's Alive

Then He got into the boat and His disciples followed Him. Without warning, a furious storm came up on the lake, so that the waves swept over the boat. But Jesus was sleeping. The disciples went and woke Him, saying, "Lord, save us! We're going to drown!"

He replied, "You of little faith, why are you so afraid?" Then He got up and rebuked the winds and the waves, and it was completely calm.

The men were amazed and asked, "What kind of man is this? Even the winds and the waves obey Him!" (Matthew 8:23–27)

Let's Dig

1 What were the disciples afraid of?

2 What kind of miracle did Jesus do? What did their fear turn into?

3 Name two "storms" in your life that you were most afraid of:

• _____   • _____

4 Does Jesus know we are going through those storms or is He sleeping?

5 Does He have the power to calm those storms? How do you know?

Mom's Turn

- Name two "storms" you have been through in the last ten years. Was Jesus "asleep in the boat" during those trials for you or did He come to your aid? How?

- Do you remember a time in your life when your picture of Jesus was that He was always asleep (and didn't care or know how to help)? How did that change?

- What do you think it takes to have a clear picture of Jesus so you can have the faith that He is able to help in time of need?

What If . . .

. . . you were one of twenty people who tried out for the school team in baseball. The coach said he would only keep fourteen. You made the first cut, but on the last day of practice when the coach trimmed the roster to his limit, your name wasn't on the list.

You considered yourself a good athlete, so getting cut was the most unexpected thing on your mind. Because you were not on the team, you not only had to face the "embarrassment" back at school, but you couldn't play baseball.

You've heard that "faith is hoping in something you haven't yet seen" (Hebrews 11:1) and "God works all things for good" (Romans 8:28), but you're having a tough time having the faith to see how God can use this "storm" for good.

What future good could possibly come from this storm?

What will you have to do to find out what that future good could be?

Now What?

To have faith that Jesus is alive and ready to help in whatever storm we're going through is not always as easy as it seems. Some people have it in their minds that to call on God when you're in trouble is a sign of weakness, but their attitude is actually a sign they don't really have faith in His power.

Tell your mom what your picture of Jesus looks like. Is He:

- awake or sleeping?
- caring or uncaring?
- powerful or powerless?
- smiling or frowning?
- alive or dead?
- happy with you or disappointed in you?
- forgiving or unforgiving?

Mom, if your child hasn't caught on to all of the qualities of God's character, now would be a good time to clear up any wrong impressions. As best you can, share what your God is like.

Overtime Challenge (300 points)

- Acts 27. What would you be thinking if you were Paul? (Use the map in your Bible to show where they were.)
- Acts 28:1–10. How did God use this storm for good?

Plant It Deep (150 points)

He replied, "You of little faith, why are you so afraid?" Then He got up and rebuked the winds and the waves, and it was completely calm. (Matthew 8:26)

13

There's Nothing Wrong with Being Sad

It's Alive

"Blessed are those who mourn, for they will be comforted." (Matthew 5:4)

Let's Dig

1 Name four things that can make you sad (mourn) for a *short* period of time.

- _____
- _____
- _____
- _____

2 Name two things that could make you sad for a *long* time—if they happened.

- _____
- _____

3 What do you think is the difference between feeling sad and feeling sorry for yourself? (Mom, you can help if needed.)

4 What helps you not to feel sad anymore?

5 Has God ever comforted you when you were sad?

Mom's Turn

- From ages eight to fifteen, what were the saddest things that happened to you? How long were you sad? What helped you to get over it?

- What are some things these days that make you feel sad?

- How has Jesus comforted you in the things that have made you sad?

What If . . .

. . . your new bike disappeared after you accidentally left it at the park.
How much time would it take to get over it?

. . . your cat had kittens, but she died in the process.
How much time would it take to get over it?

. . . a Sunday school teacher whom you really liked a lot got sick and died in the middle of the year.
How much time would it take to get over it?

Now What?

God uses time to help us get over sad circumstances. He also uses people (like parents) to help us realize that even the toughest situation can work out for the good if we love God and realize that nothing takes Him by surprise.

With your mom, try to predict the future. Write down three things that could happen in the next year or two that would make you sad. Then write down ways God could use the situation for good.

Situation #1:

How God could use it:

Situation #2:

How God could use it:

Situation #3:

How God could use it:

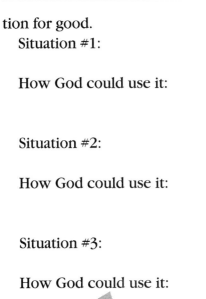

Overtime Challenge (150 points)

- Romans 8:28. Does God *cause* all things, or does He *work* all things for our good?
- 2 Corinthians 1:3–4. What is one reason God comforts us in our troubles?
- Romans 8:35–39. How has God made us more than conquerors?

Plant It Deep (200 points)

And we know that in all things God works for the good of those who love Him, who have been called according to His purpose. (Romans 8:28)

A Faith That Can
Live Forever

It's Alive

Jesus said to her, "I am the resurrection and the life. He who believes in Me will live, even though he dies; and whoever lives and believes in Me will never die. Do you believe this?" (John 11:25–26)

Let's Dig

1 When you think of death, what comes to your mind?

2 How about eternal life?

3 How much do you think God wants us to live forever?

4 Can you think of any lessons that death can teach? (Mom, you can help on this one.)

5 Do your friends ever talk about death?

Mom's Turn

- Was death something you were afraid of when you were little? Why? Why not?

- Were you ever faced with the death of a relative or friend?
- How have you learned to live life without fearing death?

What If . . .

This subject is already a little weird to talk about without throwing in a situation that hopefully won't happen. Mom, if you can think of a "what if" situation your child can relate to, feel free to use it now.

I'm going to rearrange the order a little for this one lesson. Go right to the "Overtime Challenge," OK?

Overtime Challenge (200 points)

- Genesis 1:26. In whose image was man made?
- John 4:24. What is God? Therefore, what are we?
- Hebrews 2:9. Jesus died a physical death, but He also died for whose spiritual death?
- Hebrew 2:14-15. Should we be afraid of death?

Now What?

Our bodies are earthsuits. They are only good for planet Earth. If you take an earthsuit underneath the ocean or miles high in the sky (without proper equipment), it can't function.

Our earthsuits house a spirit. That's what lives forever when our bodies don't work anymore. God knows this. That's why He had to take care of His biggest foe, death—not just physical death, but spiritual death.

Spiritual death occurs when someone hasn't taken Christ's free gift of forgiveness before his earthsuit stops working. When he refuses that gift, he is saying to God, "I don't want You to pay the penalty for my sin; I'll do it myself." Sadly, the payment is being eternally (forever) separated from God. And that's what hell is.

God doesn't want life, death, heaven, and hell to be confusing. If you still don't understand what you're really made of, what Jesus did for you, and what you have to do to be His child, ask your mom some questions and look up the passages in the "Double Overtime Challenge."

Double Overtime Challenge (50 points for each passage)

- John 5:25
- 1 Corinthians 15:12-22
- James 2:26
- Revelation 14:13
- Revelation 21:4
- Isaiah 25:8

Plant It Deep (150 points)

He will swallow up death forever, The Sovereign Lord will wipe away the tears from all faces ... (Isaiah 25:8a)

15

Ain't No Doubt about It

It's Alive

"My sheep listen to My voice; I know them, and they follow Me. I give them eternal life, and they shall never perish; no one can snatch them out of My hand. My Father, who has given them to Me, is greater than all; no one can snatch them out of My Father's hand." (John 10:27-29)

Let's Dig

1 If you've ever been lost before, how did it feel? How did it feel when you were found?

2 Is it easier to doubt the words of someone you know or someone you don't know very well?

3 Do you ever doubt you're going to heaven?

4 Though a little doubt is normal, do you think God wants you to doubt?

5 Then who are those doubts coming from?

Mom's Turn

- Have you ever been lost before? How does it feel to be lost? How did you get found or back on the right road?

- When you were a young Christian or a youngster, did you ever doubt you'd actually be living forever? Now that you're older, how are you overcoming those doubts?

- Following Jesus like a sheep is a daily battle sometimes. What do you do to help you follow more closely so that you don't doubt promises like eternal life?

What If . . .

. . . your dad decides to take you fishing. He says he's going to take you to a lake where he knows you'll catch your limit. You get up early and drive for an hour and a half. As you look around from the car window, you notice that you've taken a route and are in a place you've never seen before.

After finally arriving, you get all the tackle and poles together and head off into the woods.

"Are you sure you know where you're going, Dad?" you say to him as you follow close behind on the trail.

"Just stay close, Son," he says. "The lake is just ahead, about another fifteen minutes hike."

Though you have a few doubts, you keep following. You know your dad never lies and has always found good fishing holes for you. The best idea, you decide, is to trust that he knows what he's doing and follow closely.

If the person you went fishing with was a *friend's* dad—a total stranger—would you trust him as much when he promised you'd be going to a lake where you'd catch your limit?

What's the difference between a stranger and your dad?

How does this example relate to following God closely and believing what He says about heaven?

Now What?

Doubt usually occurs when we lose confidence in someone we should trust. That could be your mom or God. What cures doubt is for someone to prove they are faithful over a long period of time (like your mom).

God wants to show how faithful He is to you over the long haul just like your parents have done. In order for us to *know* how faithful He is, we need to (1) realize what He's already done to prove His love for us, and (2) spend time in His Word so that when Satan puts doubts in our head, we can point him back to the Bible and tell him he's lying!

Since we've talked about number two already, write down all the ways you can think of that God has proved His love for you. (It should be a pretty long list. If you get stuck, ask your mom to think of a few also.)

_____   _____

_____   _____

_____   _____

Overtime Challenge (150 points)

- John 5:24. What are the two conditions for eternal life?

- 1 John 5:12–13. If you have the Son in your life, does God want you to doubt where you will spend eternity?

- John 6:37. Does Jesus sound like He might not be telling the truth in this verse?

Plant It Deep (150 points)

He who has the Son has life; he who does not have the Son of God does not have life. (1 John 5:12)

Bonus Puzzle #3
(1,000 points)

ACROSS

6. God comforts us in our troubles so we can _____ others. (2 Corinthians 1:4)

7. "Who shall _____ us from the love of Christ?" (Romans 8:35)

8. We are made in God's _____. (Genesis 1:26)

9. God will _____ up death forever. (Isaiah 25:8)

12. "We are more than _____ through him who loved us." (Romans 8:37)

13. We start to fear when our _____ is weak. (Matthew 8:26)

14. God is _____. (John 4:24)

15. Paul and the prisoners landed on the island of _____. (Acts 28:1)

16. To have confidence that Jesus can handle our problems, we must have an accurate _____ of who Jesus is.

17. If we believe in Jesus, we will never _____. (John 11:26)

18. If we hear God's Word and believe in Jesus, we will not be _____. (John 5:24)

DOWN

1. Jesus _____ death for everyone. (Hebrews 2:9)

2. What happens to those who mourn? (Matthew 5:4)

3. Jesus is the _____ and the life. (John 11:25)

4. People are held in _____ by their fear of death. (Hebrews 2:15)

5. God wants us to _____ that we have eternal life. (1 John 5:13)

6. Our _____ should always match our mouths. (Colossians 3:9)

10. How many days was Paul at sea in the storm before they ate? (Acts 27:33)

11. "Do not _____ to each other." (Colossians 3:9)

16

Don't Let the Dam Burst!

It's Alive

It is to a man's honor to avoid strife, but every fool is quick to quarrel. (Proverbs 20:3)

Let's Dig

1 Have you ever seen quarrels that led to fights at school?

2 What are some reasons people fight?

3 Does anyone ever really win?

4 Have you ever been so mad or hurt by someone so badly that you wanted to punch him?

5 What happened?

Mom's Turn

• Talk about any quarrels that led to fights when you were in school.

- How did you feel when it was over? Did it do anything to your reputation? Did it solve the problem?

- Is fighting always avoidable? If so, how?

What If . . .

. . . an older kid was picking on your smaller brother or sister?

. . . a kid in class said in front of everyone that your answer was stupid?

. . . someone wouldn't stop calling you by a degrading nickname?

. . . a classmate dropped your math book in a mud puddle (ruining it), but wouldn't admit he did it or agree to replace it?

Now What?

Fights usually break out when someone won't do what you want him to (like apologize, fix the problem, stop an action, etc.). It starts with a quarrel or a disagreement, escalates to raised voices, which then leads to pushing and eventually to fighting (for guys especially).

While most of us try not to jump into a fight before trying to work out the problem, sometimes we get pushed to the limit, and then . . . .

You probably know that fighting is never the answer, but allowing things to hit the "quarreling" level isn't too smart, either. When are the times you quarrel with others at home? At school? In the neighborhood?

With your mom, identify the times you start to quarrel, then figure out the best strategy to deal with each circumstance (like leaving the room, counting to ten, or praying for help).

Decide what works best for you, then try it next time your anger starts to boil.

Overtime Challenge (150 points)

- Proverbs 15:1. What is the key to turning away anger?

- Romans 12:19. Whose job is it to even the score?

- Proverbs 10:19. How many words does it take to start a fight?

Plant It Deep (150 points)

It is to a man's honor to avoid strife, but every fool is quick to quarrel. (Proverbs 20:3)

No Fair!

It's Alive

The LORD abhors dishonest scales, but accurate weights are His delight. (Proverbs 11:1)

Let's Dig

1 Mom, explain what scales were used for and how they could be dishonest.

2 Name four things you think should always be done in a fair way:

- _____
- _____
- _____
- _____

3 How do you feel when things aren't handled fairly in those areas?

4 When something isn't fair, what is your response?

5 Name two things in which you are tempted not to be fair:

- _____
- _____

Mom's Turn

- Recall specific instances when people or circumstances weren't fair to you.

- How did you feel and what did you do when things weren't fair?

- How have you learned the importance of being fair? Has it always meant that others are fair with you?

What If . . .

. . . you're playing Monopoly with your family on a Friday night. As usual, your mom is "cleaning up." She knows math better and has played the game for years. She always wins! On this night, she's really winning badly. It doesn't seem fair.

What would be your natural response if Mom started winning again?

Is it fair to others that Mom always wins?

. . . you're in Sunday school and the teacher is leading a "Bible Challenge" game between the boys and the girls. Your team is losing—and it seems like the teacher isn't playing fair. Whenever a question is brought up, he calls on the other team, even though your team seems to have their hands up just as quickly.

How would you react?

Now What?

You have three choices when it comes to fairness: (1) not play fair so you can win; (2) be forced to play fair, and then grumble if you lose; or (3) play fair, accept the situation win or lose, and let fairness be the reward you're after.

Playing fair takes a lot of effort, doesn't it? When just a little unfairness means you could win, it's tempting to walk down that road. But as you can tell by the passage we started with, God likes it when we're fair—and hates it when we're not. There's nothing wrong with being competitive and trying to win, but when the cost is not playing fair, you've actually lost.

The things you mentioned in question five of "Let's Dig" are two areas in which you can start practicing fairness. What is the best way Mom can remind you of the importance of fairness when she's around (without it seeming like she's nagging)?

Overtime Challenge (150 points)

- Proverbs 1:2–3. How do you know what is fair?

- Proverbs 21:15. How can being just bring joy?

- Psalm 106:3. What is the reward for being just and fair?

Pray It Up

Dear Heavenly Father, being fair isn't always easy, especially when there are people who aren't always fair to me. But I realize that being fair makes You happy. Help me to think of Your happiness before mine in this area. And thanks that You're fair with me. You don't treat me like I deserve sometimes, but You give me breaks I don't deserve. Amen.

How to Be
Really Refreshed

It's Alive

A generous man will prosper; he who refreshes others will himself be refreshed. (Proverbs 11:25)

Let's Dig

1 What does it mean to be generous?

2 How are you generous with others?

3 When do you not feel like being generous with others?

4 What does it mean to prosper?

5 What is the reward for refreshing others?

Mom's Turn

- Have you ever believed that if you possessed something, it was yours and you didn't need to share it with others?

- Have you learned the joy that comes from giving to those who lack?

• When and how did you learn this lesson? What have been the rewards for practicing generosity?

What If . . .

. . . down the street lives an older widow lady who has to keep her yard up by herself. As you pass her house on your way home from school each day, you see that her yard is getting a little overgrown. You have some extra time after school a few days a week . . . but you're only one person, and you don't really like yard work that well.

Is this an instance you would be generous with your time? Or would you figure you're too young to worry about it?

In what ways could you help—even if it wasn't pulling all of her weeds for her?

. . . there's a children's hospital in your city. This hospital doesn't only have kids with broken legs or bad cuts on their heads; it has others with cancer and other diseases that might take their lives.

These kids have families who visit them often. But very few have kids their own ages who will come play with them or give them gifts they would really like to play with.

Do you have any extra toys, dolls, baseball cards, or books that would bring a smile to the face of someone who is hurting?

Have you thought about giving these things away before?

When would be the best time to go and visit one of these kids?

Now What?

Many of us have much more than we need—not just money, either. We have time to spare and possessions we no longer use that could brighten the life of someone less fortunate. While the goal of giving should never be to get in return, often we are the ones who really benefit from being generous. We feel better knowing we're doing something God would do.

The best part of being a Christian on this earth is doing things that God would do. It *does* feel good. Why? Because it's right! We weren't put here just to have fun; we have been blessed (refreshed) to bless (refresh) others. One cool thing about being generous is that we'll never run out of things to give. If you are giving, God sees that. He doesn't want you to run out of things to give, so He gives you more. It's amazing, but that's how it works.

Think of things you can give—time, talents, possessions, money—and pick one way you can start giving it to others.

Overtime Challenge (150 points)

- Proverbs 28:27. What happens if we close our eyes to the poor?
- Proverbs 22:2. What do we have in common with the less fortunate?
- 2 Corinthians 9:7. How should we give and what are the results?

Plant It Deep (150 points)

. . . for God loves a cheerful giver. (2 Corinthians 9:7b)

19

They Got What They Deserved

It's Alive

Do not gloat when your enemy falls; when he stumbles, do not let your heart rejoice, or the LORD will see and disapprove and turn His wrath away from him. (Proverbs 24:17–18)

Let's Dig

1. Are there people you know whom you really don't like?
2. Why don't you like them?
3. How do you feel when something bad happens to them?
4. Have you ever felt sorry for someone after he got in trouble?
5. Do you always get what you deserve when you do something wrong?

Mom's Turn

- Can you think of any times that you didn't get what you deserved when you messed up?

- Why do you think it is so tempting to gloat or rejoice when someone else gets what he deserves? How does it make you feel?

- Feeling sorry for someone—even when he's wronged us—shows we are thinking about that person the way God thinks of us. Have you learned to do that with everyone or do you still struggle with gloating over others?

What If . . .

. . . you're playing a basketball game and your team is getting beat. One reason is the other team has a really good player. The problem: though the player is good, she also plays rough, and the refs aren't calling much on her. Because it's just a grade school game, they figure they'll let the teams play. She knows that and is taking advantage.

Finally, in the third quarter she commits a foul they haven't called all game, and she argues with the ref. The next time down the court the same thing happens. This time she says something pretty mean to the ref and is given a technical foul. Her coach takes her out for the rest of the game.

How are you feeling about this person on the outside—what would you say? How about the inside? Are you glad she finally got what she deserves? Would you shake her hand after the game?

Now What?

Gloating is an attitude that can lead to words like the title of this lesson. Often we don't mean to be glad at someone else's calamity, but it just feels better because it happened to him, not us.

The reason God doesn't like gloating is because He doesn't do it Himself. When humans mess up, God isn't happy, He's sad.

He doesn't want to punish them; He wants them to turn to Him for forgiveness. Just as your parents aren't glad when you get what you deserve (because it usually isn't pleasant), God isn't either.

This is the type of quality that most people don't even try to improve. But the next time someone you don't care for gets what he deserves, think about yourself: You're not getting what you deserve from God, are you?

Overtime Challenge (200 points)

- Luke 23:41. Does God give us what we deserve?
- Job 31:29-30. What does Job call rejoicing at the calamity of others?
- Psalm 35:15. What happened to David when he was down?
- Obadiah 12. Is gloating verbal or nonverbal?

Pray It Up

Dear Heavenly Father, this is a hard attitude to learn. People who do bad things do deserve what they get. But help me never to be the judge. Give me the compassion that You have for those who deserve punishment. Help me not to gloat over them.

Thank You for not treating me the way I deserve. Thank You for forgiving my sin and calling me Your child. Amen.

20

You Won't Believe What I Got!

It's Alive

Let another praise you, and not your own mouth; someone else, and not your own lips. (Proverbs 27:2)

Let's Dig

1 Name a few people who brag about themselves. What do they brag about?

2 What are you thinking when you hear someone tell you or others how good they are at something?

3 When people talk about things they've done or seen, is that bragging?

4 Are there some good things to brag about?

5 When are you most tempted to brag?
- ❏ when you've done something good
- ❏ when you've seen something no one else has seen
- ❏ when others are bragging first

❑ when you're not getting enough attention at home or with your friends

❑ when a family member or friend has done something cool

Mom's Turn

• What are some things you could have bragged about when you were a kid? Did you very often?

• Why do you think people brag? Describe the type of person who brags the most.

• Are there good things to brag about? When is the right time to praise something?

What If . . .

. . . you and your best friend both want a new bike for Christmas. You talk to each other about what kind you told your parents you wanted. Both of you are sure they'll get one for you. But when Christmas morning comes, *you* don't get one. About noon, your friend calls to ask what kind you got. When you say you didn't get one, he tells you the kind he got. "It's even a better one than I asked for!" he says. He goes on and on about how great it is.

How would you feel about your friend?

What would you have done if it was you who got the bike, instead of your friend?

Now What?

Boasting or bragging is normal. Nobody wants to go through life being unnoticed. If people don't give us the attention we need, we tend to hang a sign that says "notice me" by telling them something we did or something we got. As you're growing, that's OK to do. But as you mature (Mom, explain that word), bragging is actually a sign that you aren't very secure—that perhaps you don't like yourself just like you are.

Right now, tell Mom how you feel about yourself. Answer each of these questions: Do you think you're a pretty neat kid? Are you getting enough attention from your parents or your friends? Do you sometimes feel like no one knows you exist? Do you know how much God cares about you?

When you feel secure, you no longer need to boast. Instead, you'll be content to wait for others to praise you for who you are and things you do.

Overtime Challenge (200 points)

- James 4:13–17. What shouldn't we boast about? Why?

- Ephesians 2:8–9. What gift shouldn't we boast about?

- James 3:5. How can boasting be harmful?

Pray It Up

Dear Lord, You have shown me how valuable I am by coming to earth and dying on a cross for me. I realize in a small way how important I am to You. I don't want to be a bragger my whole life, constantly looking for others to notice me. I want to be secure and like me for me. Would You help me do that? Thanks. Amen.

Bonus Puzzle #4
(1,000 Points)

```
M  F  K  W  O  Z  O  I  B  R  A  G  Q  U  E
R  E  F  R  E  S  H  E  D  C  N  E  P  O  R
E  J  C  O  M  P  A  S  S  I  O  N  U  M  A
W  V  H  O  N  O  R  E  L  K  I  E  P  A  C
A  E  Q  U  I  S  M  A  Z  F  T  R  L  N  C
R  F  F  F  A  S  F  I  O  T  A  O  L  G  U
D  I  O  D  T  E  U  O  V  I  T  U  M  E  R
T  R  R  R  E  S  L  W  S  A  U  S  H  R  A
S  T  T  W  G  S  E  E  H  K  P  N  D  L  T
E  S  U  Z  E  I  E  N  M  K  E  O  R  E  E
N  W  N  T  S  O  V  R  H  F  R  P  O  R  M
O  W  A  S  T  N  X  E  V  T  Z  E  G  R  J
H  Y  T  A  H  S  H  N  N  E  A  Y  A  A  V
S  O  E  O  G  J  P  C  H  E  E  R  F  U  L
I  X  H  B  I  M  F  E  O  P  S  B  W  Q  K
D  W  Q  U  F  A  I  R  N  E  S  S  D  I  P
```

ACCURATE	FIGHTS	POSSESSIONS
ANGER	FOOL	PRAISE
BOAST	FORGIVENESS	QUARREL
BRAG	FORTUNATE	REFRESHED
CHEERFUL	GENEROUS	REPUTATION
COMPASSION	GLOAT	REWARD
DESERVE	HARMFUL	STRIFE
DISHONEST	HONOR	WRATH
FAIRNESS	POOR	

21

Don't Walk Crooked!

It's Alive

The man of integrity walks securely, but he who takes crooked paths will be found out. (Proverbs 10:9)

Let's Dig

1 The dictionary defines *integrity* like this: "The quality or state of being of sound moral principle; uprightness, honesty, and sincerity." Does this say you have to be perfect?

2 Does this mean you're upright only if you get a reward for it?

3 Does this mean you're honest only when there are no consequences?

4 Does this mean you're sincere only when others are?

5 What are possible rewards for having integrity?

Mom's Turn

- What did the word *integrity* mean to you when you were growing up?

- What does it mean to you now? (How important is integrity for you as an adult?)

- How does someone learn to have integrity? What do you think is the reward for having it?

What If . . .

. . . you were known as a student who could be trusted. You worked hard at your studies and didn't cheat. One Friday, you looked over at the paper of your neighbor during a math test. You didn't mean to see his answer on number twelve, but you noticed it was different than yours. You rechecked your answer and found you had made a mistake, so you changed your answer. At afternoon recess, your teacher mentioned she was shocked to see you looking at the paper of another student, and asked you if you were cheating.

What would a person of integrity do? (Circle one.)

a. Deny he looked or cheated.

b. Admit he looked but didn't cheat.

c. Say to the teacher, "What are you talking about?"

d. Admit he looked on question twelve and offer to have that question marked wrong.

e. Admit he looked on question twelve and offer to take an "F" on the test.

What feels better the next day: getting an "A" or a passing grade, or having a clear conscience?

What's easier to do: take congratulations from your parents for doing well on a test you cheated on, or admitting you cheated on one question and being willing to face whatever consequences your teacher or parents think best?

Now What?

Why is the right thing so hard to do sometimes? Because we don't often get the reward we want for doing it. What we want is the immediate reward of praise from our parents or a good grade from a teacher. What God wants for you, however, is the long-term reward of being a person with integrity. Integrity often has short-term "consequences" (when we make mistakes and have to own up to them), but it is a much better reward.

In fact, the passage we started with says that those without integrity will eventually be found out anyway. That makes it even more important to pursue integrity.

This character quality takes practice. It also takes some maturity (there's that word again). You have to be the type who wants the *bigger* rewards of a clean conscience and a good name, instead of the *smaller* reward you can receive by being dishonest.

So what do you do now? Maybe it's time to decide if integrity is a word you want people to use when they think of you.

Overtime Challenge (150 points)

- Proverbs 28:18. How many actions does it take to fall?

- Isaiah 33:15–16. What is the reward for walking rightly over a long period of time?

- Matthew 10:26. What does this verse emphasize?

Pray It Up

Dear Heavenly Father, though I can't see the big *reward I'll receive for having integrity, I'm beginning to understand how important it is. I know I can't be perfect all the time— and I know that's not what You expect—but without the courage that comes from You to accept responsibility, I will make poor choices. Give me that courage, Lord, and help me to keep my eyes on You—and my own paper! Amen.*

22

"Don't Worry, I Won't Tell Anyone"

It's Alive

A gossip betrays a confidence, but a trustworthy man keeps a secret. (Proverbs 11:13)

Let's Dig

1. Do you like telling friends things you know about others?
2. Do you like hearing things about friends that not very many people know?
3. Do you like it when a friend tells someone else something about you you didn't want him to know?
4. Are you good at keeping secrets?
5. When you gossip about others, are you usually saying good things or not-so-good things about them?

Mom's Turn

- Though this is a tough topic to try to remember anything on, give it a try.

- If you can't think of an example of when you gossiped or when gossip from others hurt you, ask your husband. He might be able to remember a few examples from his life.

- How are you tempted to gossip now as an adult? Does gossip happen in the church? How does it help or hurt?

What If . . .

. . . a good friend told you his parents were getting a divorce and she may have to move. She didn't tell you *not* to tell anyone else.

Would it be gossip to tell other people what was going on? Should you ask her the question, "Do you want me to keep quiet about this, or is it OK to tell others if they ask?"

. . . you told your best friend about a girl you liked a little (or boy if you're a girl, of course). It's not like you wanted her for a girlfriend; you just liked her a little more than other girls.

Would you want him to tell that girl what you said?
Would you want him to tell a friend of that girl what you said?
Would you want him to tell any of your friends what you said?
What should you say to him so he wouldn't tell anyone else?
What would you say if he did tell anyone else?

Now What?

Let's admit it: gossiping about others is fun. And hearing gossip about others is also pretty fun. But it's not so fun to be the one who's gossiped about, is it? Why? Because often the gossip isn't true, or it's something you didn't want others to know, right?

So why do we gossip about others when we wouldn't want it done to us?

Good question! It's almost like we can't help it.

Gossip is a lot like sin. That is, since we're human, we *will* sin.

And since we're human, we *will* gossip. Whenever we gossip, it's a good reminder of how sinful we really are.

But unlike sin, we can eventually get this area under control—if we want. First, we need to ask the Lord to remind us when we're gossiping. Second, we need to realize the consequences of doing it (we could lose friends!). Third, we need to recognize when others are gossiping and ask them to stop.

Two good rules to go by are:

1. *If the person I'm talking to isn't part of the solution to helping someone, he doesn't need to know it.*

2. *If I'm not part of the solution to the situation being told to me, I don't need to hear it.* (No matter how fun it may be to know about something.)

This week, pick one person you have a tendency to gossip to (or to listen to gossip from) and practice keeping your mouth and ears closed.

Overtime Challenge (150 points)

- Proverbs 20:19. Should we hang around with a gossip?
- Romans 1:28-30. Why is gossip mixed in with all these other bad things?
- Proverbs 16:28. What is a consequence of being a gossip?

Pray It Up

Dear Lord, remind me how destructive it is to gossip and to listen to gossip. It's so tempting to do both, but I know You can give the strength to overcome any *temptation. I want that strength in this area. Amen.*

23

Pride and Disgrace

It's Alive

When pride comes, then comes disgrace, but with humility comes wisdom. (Proverbs 11:2)

Let's Dig

1 Name two things you are glad you can do well:

• _____   • _____

2 Is it OK to feel good about things you can do well?

3 How do you judge whether you are too proud?

4 What does being humble mean to you?

5 Would people call you humble, quiet, or neither?

Mom's Turn

• What were some things about yourself you felt good about when you were growing up?

• How did you show those feelings?

• Name some ways pride can be disgraceful.

What If . . .

. . . you know most of the Bible stories talked about in Sunday school, and whenever competitions are held, you usually know the answer. This is something you've worked hard to learn. It's OK to feel good about it. But there is a way to be humble about the fact that you know them.

How can you practice being humble in this situation?

. . . in soccer, you have a strong leg. It seems like since you were small you've always been able to kick the ball a long way. When you play at recess, kids can't believe how far and accurately you can kick it. While some of this skill comes from practice, a lot of the reason for it is because you were just born a good athlete.

If you're proud about an attribute you had nothing to do with, are you *more* or *less* likely to be disgraced?

Now What?

Not all pride is bad. But pride in appearance or power is what got the serpent (Satan) kicked out of the Garden of Eden. That type of pride God can't stand. Why? Whenever your pride makes you forget about God, that means you're trying to replace Him, trying to be God of your own life. That's why it's so destructive.

Feeling good about yourself for a job well done isn't bad. And being proud of an accomplishment (yours or someone else's), is OK, too. Only pride that forgets about God is destructive.

Is there anything in your life that you are *too* proud about? If so, how can you begin to deflect those feelings of pride to include the One who made you?

Overtime Challenge (150 points)

• Proverbs 13:10. What does pride hatch?

- Proverbs 8:13. What should we hate and what does the Lord hate?
- Proverbs 22:4. What are the rewards of humility?

Plant It Deep (150 points)

He has showed you, O man, what is good. And what does the LORD require of you? To act justly and to love mercy and to walk humbly with your God. (Micah 6:8)

24

Which Crowd Do I Choose?

It's Alive

My son, if sinners entice you, do not give in to them.
(Proverbs 1:10)

Let's Dig

1 Is there a crowd at school that always gets into trouble?

2 What do they do?

3 Are they the popular or unpopular kids?

4 Have you ever felt like you wanted to be in that group?

5 Have they ever tried to get you in?

Mom's Turn

- Talk about a few of the groups or kids in school who always seemed to get in trouble. What did they do?

- Were you ever a part of one of those groups?

- Do you recall what the home life of these kids was? Why do you think they acted the way they did?

What If . . .

. . . it's after school, and you're walking home with a few of your friends. Just ahead of you are a couple of older kids who are popular (though not always well-liked—Mom, what's the difference?). They turn around and start talking to you. Then they start talking about an old lady up the block who has a strawberry patch in her back yard. They say they're going to sneak back there and grab a few strawberries. They want you to come along. Two of your friends think it's a good idea . . . and you *are* a little hungry.

Are you tempted to join them? What would be so wrong with following along?

Now What?

There are two ways kids get into trouble: (1) by entering or befriending a group of kids who are known to like to get into it; (2) by accidentally allowing their own group of friends to influence them to do something they know is wrong. The second one is what usually happens. Because the group decides to do something, no one wants to be the only one to say no.

There's a character quality you need to want for yourself: COURAGE. When you are able to stand for what you know is right, this is what happens:

1. You feel good about yourself. Doing what's right *feels* good.

2. Your conscience is clear—with God and your parents. You don't have to lie, and you don't have to confess.

3. You can be happy with yourself.

100

4. Others will follow. That's right. Most don't want to do wrong, but they just don't want to look weak, so they give in. The strong one, however, is the person who can say, "No, let's do something else." Sure there might be some pressure or some kidding for being a "goody-goody," but it will soon go away.

5. Your friends *will* respect you. They may be mad temporarily, but over time they will wish they had what you had—COURAGE.

If there is a particular activity your friends like to do that you know is wrong, talk with Mom about potential responses you can give when you feel pressured to go along.

Overtime Challenge (150 points)

- 1 Corinthians 15:33. What is "good character"?

- Proverbs 14:22. Where do "evil plotters" go?

- Proverbs 29:25. When we're faced with following the wrong crowd, we're usually afraid of what they'll do or think. What is the cure?

Pray It Up

Dear Heavenly Father, I want to be a person of courage. I don't want to give in to the pressure from the crowd. Remind me about the courage I want, and help me to lead and not follow. Amen.

25

Just Kidding!

It's Alive

A man who lacks judgment derides his neighbor, but a man of understanding holds his tongue. (Proverbs 11:12)

Let's Dig

1 Who are the "put-down kings" at your school?

2 Are they liked or not liked?

3 Why do people put others down ("deride their neighbors")?

4 Do you have the habit of putting others down, or can you hold your tongue?

5 Name three reasons why people put others down:

- _____

- _____

- _____

Mom's Turn

- What did kids get put down for when you were in school? Who were the ones who would do it?

- What were you like? Were you an "arrow" or the "target"?

- What type of person do you hope your child becomes: someone who is quick with his tongue and can put others in their place, or someone who knows how to hold his tongue? Why?

What If . . .

Pick the response that best describes what you would probably do if you heard someone being put down (please be honest).

a. Keep my mouth shut

b. Laugh along

c. Join in a little

d. Join in a lot

e. Tell others to cut it out

f. Try to make the person feel better later by assuring him his tormentors were jerks—and he is OK.

What if...

...a person who didn't have the same color skin as you was being called names? _____

...one of your good friends was being put down because of what he was wearing that day? _____

...you were at the lunch table, and an overweight girl sat down with a big sack lunch, then two guys immediately started to make fun of her? _____

. . . a kid who couldn't keep up during long-distance running in P.E. was being called a "wimp" by some of the better athletes?

Now What?

Put-downs come in all shapes and sizes. Many seem harmless, especially if they are aimed at friends (friends who can give it back as quick as it's given to them). The ones that are targeted at someone who can't defend himself, however, are especially cruel.

Is *any* put-down safe, though?

No.

It usually hurts the other person (even if he acts like he can take it). And it shows the one flinging the cutting words how small he really is. That's right. A put-down king is just someone who doesn't like himself, so he deflects attention away from himself and puts down someone else.

Have you ever thought of being the "put-up king"? That's someone who finds good things about others and makes sure everyone knows about those good things. What would it take for you to start practicing that? Develop a plan with Mom for one or two people you can start to "put up." Then do it!

Overtime Challenge (150 points)

- Proverbs 12:14. What will good, fruitful lips give?

- Proverbs 10:31–32. What does the mouth of the righteous bring out? The mouth of the perverse?

- Ephesians 4:29. What type of speech should come from our mouths?

Plant It Deep (150 points)

"He who guards his lips guards his life, but he who speaks rashly will come to ruin." (Proverbs 13:3)

Bonus Puzzle #5
(1,000 Points)

```
E  M  Y  T  R  O  U  B  L  E  J  N  M  S  G
N  O  C  L  I  P  S  T  E  G  R  A  T  I  U
T  R  L  U  F  R  E  W  O  P  A  E  E  N  A
I  A  E  G  A  R  U  O  C  Q  R  C  X  C  R
C  L  A  V  M  U  M  Y  Y  C  O  I  P  E  D
E  S  R  A  C  E  L  H  E  N  J  L  D  R  S
R  P  W  R  K  H  R  S  S  Y  A  R  T  E  B
B  T  R  E  S  P  E  C  T  S  K  G  B  J  D
C  I  W  A  H  M  I  I  Y  K  I  M  S  U  S
R  L  R  P  P  E  R  V  E  R  S  E  D  S  E
O  I  R  O  N  G  J  C  R  U  E  L  L  T  D
O  M  E  C  E  N  L  G  R  U  I  N  O  L  I
K  U  E  T  R  U  S  T  W  O  R  T  H  Y  R
E  H  N  P  E  U  G  N  O  T  W  H  M  L  E
D  I  S  G  R  A  C  E  Q  U  N  D  D  U  D
```

BETRAYS	GUARDS	RASHLY
CLEAR	HOLDS	RESPECT
CONSCIENCE	INTEGRITY	RUIN
COURAGE	JUSTLY	SECRET
CROOKED	LIPS	SINCERE
CROWD	MERCY	TARGET
CRUEL	MORALS	TONGUE
DERIDES	PERVERSE	TROUBLE
DISGRACE	POWERFUL	TRUSTWORTHY
ENTICE	PRIDE	

Suggested Prize List

These are only suggestions for prizes. If a prize is too expensive to offer, the parent has the option to choose different prizes ... as long as the child agrees to them, of course!

Prize List A (for 1,500 points or more)

- Go out for ice cream some weekday evening—just you and Mom.

- Rent a video and watch it together.

- Take a trip to the local library to look for some great books.

- Eat lunch at a favorite fast-food spot.

- Go through old photo albums together and make a collage of pictures of just you two to put in a special wall hanging.

- Buy a model and put it together, or a paint-by-number painting and paint it together.

- Walk to the store together to buy some junk food.

- Learn a new board game.

- Take a long drive.

- Make breakfast together for the whole family.

- Learn a new card game.

- Go to Dairy Queen for a Mister Misty.

- Your choice: _____

- Your choice: _____

- Your choice: _____

Prize List B (for 2,500 points or more)

- Get two packs of premium sports cards.
- Go to the toy store and buy a new game to play together.
- Go to a Christian bookstore together, listen to some new tapes, and then pick out the one you want.
- See a movie together.
- Play miniature golf together.
- Learn how to play tennis.
- Go on an all-day hike.
- Start a new collection.
- Take a trip to the zoo. (Maybe you can take the whole family!)
- Your choice: _____
- Your choice: _____
- Your choice: _____

Prize List C (for 5,000 points or more)

- Take a long bike ride and picnic with Mom.
- Have Mom take you on a fifteen-dollar shopping spree at the local mall.
- Go for pizza and games at Chuck E. Cheese.
- Go bowling together once a month for three straight months.
- Take a trip to a sports card show with fifteen dollars from Mom.
- Skip church and go for a drive (just kidding).

- Make a fort or a playhouse.
- Your choice: _____
- Your choice: _____
- Your choice: _____

Prize List D (for 10,000 points or more)

- Get your allowance raised by fifty cents a week for a whole year.
- Take a one-day "outdoors" trip with Mom.
- Have breakfast with Mom once a month for six months at a favorite breakfast spot.
- Go to a pro sports game together (getting there early enough to watch them practice).
- Go camping together for one night and a day.
- Your choice: _____
- Your choice: _____
- Your choice: _____

Prize List E (for 15,000 points or more)

- Get your allowance raised by one dollar a week for a whole year.
- Get a new Bible Nintendo game.
- Buy new tennis shoes or an outfit that you've wanted.
- Take six weeks of golf or tennis lessons together (depending on the price).
- Go camping together for a weekend.

- Buy a new Game Boy cartridge.
- Your choice: _____
- Your choice: _____
- Your choice: _____

Bonus Puzzle Answers

Bonus Puzzle #1

```
                    ¹W
 ²A  N  X  I  O  U  ³S       ⁴M              ⁵F
                     S       ⁶T  R  O  U  B  L  E  D
                     D       O               E
                     O       N           ⁷J  E  S  U  S
 ⁸W      ⁹T  E  M  P  L  E    I               C
  O       E          S       V          ¹⁰E  A  R  T  H  L  Y
  R       S          S       E      ¹¹G
  R       T          N                   O
  Y              ¹²S  T  E  A  D  F  A  S  T
  I          ¹³P     K                   P
  N           R      E                   E
 ¹⁴G  E  N  E  R  O  U  S  L  Y          L
              P
              A
              R
              E
```

Bonus Puzzle #2

```
E  R  N  D  N  A  S  U  F  F  E  R  I  N  G  F  K
H  O  I  L  U  F  H  T  I  A  F  A  R  B  D  O  P
A  C  S  C  Z  P  I  H  S  W  O  L  L  E  F  R  Y
N  K  O  E  C  R  P  E  R  D  A  N  G  E  R  F  D
T  Q  U  A  C  E  W  K  L  C  I  N  S  S  P  E  E
S  B  F  E  C  R  R  O  P  E  A  X  E  N  K  I  S
E  G  O  D  B  R  E  A  T  H  E  D  R  O  I  T  S
N  Y  U  N  O  L  C  T  I  C  N  E  V  I  M  U  A
O  L  N  P  E  C  K  S  W  O  J  P  I  S  O  D  R
H  E  D  M  G  E  E  A  H  M  P  P  C  S  S  E  R
S  Y  A  S  T  R  D  R  N  M  E  I  E  E  B  E  A
I  C  T  L  Y  P  I  L  V  A  Q  U  I  S  E  N  B
D  R  I  C  H  E  S  E  E  N  U  Q  Y  S  T  B  M
T  O  O  R  R  O  B  I  F  D  R  E  M  O  R  S  E
C  O  N  T  E  N  T  O  T  S  U  R  T  P  A  N  O
P  D  E  R  E  D  N  A  W  P  L  E  N  T  Y  T  B
```

Bonus Puzzle #3

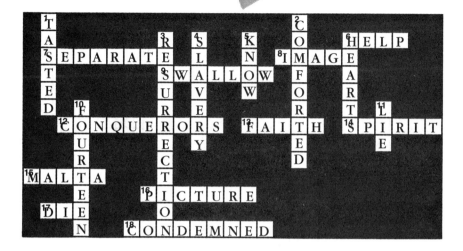

Bonus Puzzle #4

```
M  F  K  W  O  Z  O  I  B  R  A  G  Q  U  E
R  E  F  R  E  S  H  E  D  C  N  E  P  O  R
E  J  C  O  M  P  A  S  S  I  O  N  U  M  A
W  V  H  O  N  O  R  E  L  K  I  E  P  A  C
A  E  Q  U  I  S  M  A  Z  F  T  R  L  N  C
R  F  F  F  A  S  F  I  O  T  A  O  L  G  U
D  I  O  D  T  E  U  O  V  I  T  U  M  E  R
T  R  R  R  E  S  L  W  S  A  U  S  H  R  A
S  T  T  W  G  S  E  E  H  K  P  N  D  L  T
E  S  U  Z  E  I  E  N  M  K  E  O  R  E  E
N  W  N  T  S  O  V  R  H  F  R  P  O  R  M
O  W  A  S  S  T  N  X  E  V  T  Z  E  G  R  J
H  Y  T  A  H  S  H  N  N  E  A  Y  A  A  V
S  O  E  O  G  J  P  C  H  E  E  R  F  U  L
I  X  H  B  I  M  F  E  O  P  S  B  W  Q  K
D  W  Q  U  F  A  I  R  N  E  S  S  D  I  P
```

Bonus Puzzle #5

```
E   M   Y   T   R   O   U   B   L   E   J   N   M   S   G
N   O   C   L   I   P   S   T   E   G   R   A   T   I   U
T   R   L   U   F   R   E   W   O   P   A   E   E   N   A
I   A   E   G   A   R   U   O   C   Q   R   C   X   C   R
C   L   A   V   M   U   M   Y   Y   C   O   I   P   E   D
E   S   R   A   C   E   L   H   E   N   J   L   D   R   S
R   P   W   R   K   H   R   S   S   Y   A   R   T   E   B
B   T   R   E   S   P   E   C   T   S   K   G   B   J   D
C   I   W   A   H   M   I   I   Y   K   I   M   S   U   S
R   L   R   P   P   E   R   V   E   R   S   E   D   S   E
O   I   R   O   N   G   J   C   R   U   E   L   L   T   D
O   M   E   C   E   N   L   G   R   U   I   N   O   L   I
K   U   E   T   R   U   S   T   W   O   R   T   H   Y   R
E   H   N   P   E   U   G   N   O   T   W   H   M   L   E
D   I   S   G   R   A   C   E   Q   U   N   D   D   U   D
```

Scripture Passages Index

Passage	Chapter	Main	Memory
Proverbs 20:19	22		
Proverbs 21:15	17		
Proverbs 22:2	18		
Proverbs 22:4	23		
Proverbs 24:17–18	19	yes	
Proverbs 26:24–26	11		
Proverbs 27:2	20	yes	
Proverbs 28:18	21		
Proverbs 28:27	18		
Proverbs 29:25	24		
Isaiah 25:8	14		yes
Isaiah 26:3	1		yes
Isaiah 33:15–16	21		
Jeremiah 9:4-6	11		
Micah 6:8	23		yes
Obadiah 12	19		
Matthew 4:5–7	5	yes	
Matthew 5:4	13	yes	
Matthew 7:9–11	2	yes	
Matthew 7:12	9	yes	
Matthew 7:24–27	6	yes	yes (v. 24)
Matthew 8:23–27	12	yes	yes (v. 26)
Matthew 10:26	21		
Matthew 15:8	11	yes	
Matthew 19:23–24	9	yes	
Matthew 21:28–31a	8	yes	
Matthew 26:20–22	10	yes	
Matthew 27:3–5	10		
Mark 8:38	4		
Luke 2:52	3	yes	
Luke 9:25	9	yes	

Passage	Chapter	Main	Memory
Philippians 4:6–7	1		
Philippians 4:11-13	9		yes (v. 12b)
Colossians 3:2	3		
Colossians 3:9–10	11		
1 Timothy 1:12	7		
1 Timothy 6:6–10	9		
2 Timothy 1:8	10		yes
2 Timothy 3:14–17	6		
Hebrews 2:9	14		
Hebrews 2:15	14		
Hebrews 5:7–9	8		
Hebrews 13:5	9		
1 Peter 1:13	3		
James 1:5–8	2		
James 2:26	14		
James 3:5	20		
James 4:3	2		
James 4:13–17	20		
1 John 3:21–22	2		
1 John 5:3	8		yes
1 John 5:12–13	15		yes (v. 12)
Revelation 14:13	14		
Revelation 21:4	14		

Point Totals Scorecard

Section One

	Page	"Done" Points	Bonus Points	Total
1. Give It Up—and Don't Take It Back!	1	500 +	___ =	___
2. Praying for Stones and Snakes	5	500 +	___ =	___
3. Keeping Your Balance	9	500 +	___ =	___
4. What Do You Love Most?	13	500 +	___ =	___
5. Doing Stupid Stuff	17	500 +	___ =	___
Bonus Puzzle #1	20	(750 possible) +	___	
Grand Total				___
Points Redeemed				– ___
Points Carried Over				___

Section Two

	Page	"Done" Points	Bonus Points	Total
6. How Solid Is Your Rock?	23	500 +	___ =	___
7. Can You Be Trusted?	27	500 +	___ =	___
8. It's the Heart That Counts	31	500 +	___ =	___
9. How Much Is Enough?	35	500 +	___ =	___
10. Would You Betray a Friend?	39	500 +	___ =	___
Bonus Puzzle #2	43	(1,000 possible) +	___	
Carry-over Points from Section One			+	___
Grand Total				___
Points Redeemed				– ___
Points Carried Over				___

Section Three

	Page	"Done" Points	Bonus Points	Total
11. Tickling Someone's Ears	45	500 +	___ =	___
12. Who You Gonna Call?	49	500 +	___ =	___
13. There's Nothing Wrong with Being Sad	53	500 +	___ =	___
14. A Faith That Can Live Forever	57	500 +	___ =	___
15. Ain't No Doubt about It	61	500 +	___ =	___
Bonus Puzzle #3	64	(1,000 possible) +	___	
Carry-over Points from Section Two			+	___
Grand Total				___
Points Redeemed			–	___
Points Carried Over				___

Section Four

	Page	"Done" Points	Bonus Points	Total
16. Don't Let the Dam Burst!	67	500 +	___ =	___
17. No Fair!	71	500 +	___ =	___
18. How to Be Really Refreshed	75	500 +	___ =	___
19. They Got What They Deserved	79	500 +	___ =	___
20. You Won't Believe What I Got!	83	500 +	___ =	___
Bonus Puzzle #4	86	(1,000 possible) +	___	
Carry-over Points from Section Three			+	___
Grand Total				___
Points Redeemed			–	___
Points Carried Over				___

Section Five

	Page	"Done" Points	Bonus Points	Total
21. Don't Walk Crooked!	*87*	500 +	___ =	___
22. "Don't Worry, I Won't Tell Anyone"	*91*	500 +	___ =	___
23. Pride and Disgrace	*95*	500 +	___ =	___
24. Which Crowd Do I Choose?	*99*	500 +	___ =	___
25. Just Kidding!	*103*	500 +	___ =	___
Bonus Puzzle #5	*106*	(1,000 possible) +	___	

Carry-over Points from Section Four + ___

Grand Total ___

Points Redeemed – ___

Points Carried Over ___

Plan It Deep Review (50 points each)

Isaiah 26:3	_____	Romans 1:16	_____
Matthew 7:24	_____	Luke 16:10	_____
1 John 5:3	_____	Philippians 4:12b	_____
2 Timothy 1:8a	_____	Matthew 8:26	_____
Romans 8:28	_____	Isaiah 25:8a	_____
1 John 5:12	_____	Proverbs 20:3	_____
2 Corinthians 9:7b	_____	Micah 6:8	_____
Proverbs 13:3	_____		

Total Points _____ = _____

Total Points Left to Redeem _____ = _____